FEARLESS

WRITTEN BY MIRRA TODD

CURRENCY PLAYS

First published in 2012
by Currency Press Pty Ltd,
PO Box 2287, Strawberry Hills, NSW, 2012, Australia
enquiries@currency.com.au
www.currency.com.au
in association with Milk Crate Theatre
Reprinted in 2014

NATIONAL LIBRARY OF AUSTRALIA CIP DATA

Author:	Todd, Mirra.
Title:	Fearless / Mirra Todd.
ISBN:	9780868199665 (pbk.)
Other Authors/Contributors:	
	Sean Barker; Owen Gill; Michael Godlee; Christa Hughes; Robin Levy; Ray Morgan; Wayne Schmidt; John Turanga; Daryl Wallis; Bridget Wood and Sarah Woods.
Series:	Current theatre series.
Subject:	Loneliness—Drama.
Dewey Number:	A822.4

Typeset by Dean Nottle for Currency Press.
Cover design by by Gillian Thomas.
Cover image: Wayne Schmidt; Michael Godlee; Bridget Wood; John Turanga; Owen Gill and Ray Morgan (photo: Tim Jones Photography).

Contents

Introduction   *v*

Inside the Hell Room
   Mirra Todd   *ix*

FEARLESS   1

Currency Press acknowledges the Traditional Owners of the Country on which
we live and work. We pay our respects to all Aboriginal and Torres Strait
Islander Elders, past and present.

INTRODUCTION

Milk Crate Theatre collaborates with an Ensemble of people who have experienced homelessness and / or social marginalisation to create theatre that creates change. Since 2000, when the idea of Milk Crate Theatre was passionately conceived, the company has considered itself to be both a community and a theatre company, a safe place to connect and create theatre that is transformative for those that make it and those that engage with it. An intersection between the homeless and socially marginalised experience and that of the wider community.

Fearless utilised Milk Crate Theatre's unique creative process of peer-to-peer mentoring between associate artists and the Ensemble to generate an extraordinarily authentic and innovative production. The content was developed with and from the Ensemble through consultation and several creative developments over a twelve-month process, with a clear ethical mandate to not expose individual's stories within the work itself. We honour the fact that whilst their life experience may inform them, it must not define them.

Theatre is by its very nature a collaborative and creative medium. A writer can sit at their typewriter alone to write their novel, a painter can dip their brush into a palette in utter isolation and begin their masterpiece, a sculptor can mould the clay without support from anyone else, a photographer can capture an image without another person even being aware of the moment it happened, but thankfully not so in theatre. Theatre can only tell its stories through artistic collaboration. Theatre, to debunk the myth, is simply a series of offers that are built upon—from the original idea, through to the scripting, casting, set, lighting and costume design elements being added until the final offer of a 'play' to the audience. Even the word play itself speaks to the fun element inherent in theatre. What then are the particular stories Milk Crate Theatre is interested in investigating? The stories of the other, of the people who live on the edge of our societal shadow, that we everyday Australians can innocently walk past, step over, or maybe not even glimpse. They are penumbra's all. If we are honest, it is in fact the marginalised of any society that speaks to the very heart of its culture and its core community values, as their stories reflect its social fallibility. Their stories and our exploration of the themes inherent within their stories remain critical to our culture's maturation, integrity and sustainability.

It's also crucial to understand that when individuals initially link in with Milk Crate Theatre their experience has often been, due to ongoing mental, financial, social, familial or personal issues and isolation. So a process that demands collaboration is compelling and threatening in equal measure. The initial step into one of our workshops is unto itself an absolute act of bravery.

On any given night 16,000 people are homeless in Sydney alone. Homelessness can affect anyone at anytime but is more prevalent in already marginalised communities including people who have a lived experienced of mental illness, people with disabilities and Indigenous Australians. Homelessness is not just 'houselessness'. Experiencing homelessness means not having stable, secure housing or a place to call home. It is comprised of people who are 'sleeping rough', couch surfing, living with family and friends, residing at boarding houses, shelters and refuges.

Milk Crate Theatre views homelessness as a transitional state as well as a chronic state, a vulnerable state, one that can be preventable: one that can't be reversible and within wider society shouldn't exist. Whilst some people choose homelessness, many don't and many experience homelessness but don't identify as 'being homeless'. In many ways it is extremely complex, it is very personal yet it is also open to the public, it can be confronting but just as easily ignored and dismissed.

At its most practical, Milk Crate Theatre is a safe space to have fun, meet people, learn new skills and to engage with the imaginative self. But we are far more. We are a collaboration between actors, artists, welfare services and community members working with passion, commitment and integrity. Our potency lies within our unique mix of individuals and our creative collaboration: in working together.

Fearless represents the company's growing aspirations to create work that is vibrant and provocative, authentic and of the highest artistic value. It is a means for the Ensemble to represent the strength in collaboration between the welfare and arts community and advocate for the wider issues of homelessness and social marginalisation. It stands as Milk Crate Theatre's first company production to be presented as an externally programmed season of work in an acclaimed arts venue. It has created the first real opportunity for the Ensemble to be paid as professional actors and/or theatre makers, and we deliver a program around employment and financial management as part of this process.

Fearless also stands as a piece of work that can advocate for the many real and apparent issues confronting us as a greater society. Driven by the very community in which it is based, it seeks to inform policy and systemic change, in individuals, organisations, governments and decision makers.

INSIDE THE HELL ROOM

MIRRA TODD

Fearless is a play born out of a true partnership between an extraordinary company of creatively brave artists, it is a story told through and from many different eyes. The play began its genesis when I posed three simple questions to the Ensemble (people who have experienced homeless and/or social marginalisation) at the beginning of 2011, my first year as Artistic Director of Milk Crate Theatre.

1. What is something you don't understand about yourself?
2. What is something you don't understand about the world you live in?
3. What is an issue or theme you would like to profoundly explore?

After distilling the various remnants of the responses a clear premise emerged, that of loneliness. We now had a theme, but one that was epic in scope and yet private and personally exposing in its intensity. Where to begin? As always, Milk Crate Theatre seeks creative provocateurs, individuals happy to push the social, political and theatrical framework, and so for two weeks composer Daryl Wallis, singer Christa Hughes, actors Sean Barker, Lucy Bell and Tony Cogin, myself as playwright and from the Ensemble; Murray, Robin, Rob, Fabiola, John T, John M and Michael, all led by workshop director Naomi Edwards explored the many portals of loneliness.

After two weeks we felt we were just really beginning to glimpse the breadth and possibility of our theme, but several things became clear. Loneliness has been around since the dawn of time. It takes many forms, temptress, bully, friend, consoler, liberator and tormentor. It also feels like some 'thing' is missing: a lacking if you will. We learned it fuels addiction; depression; anxiety and psychosis, that it embraces shame with a welcoming kiss and thwarts dreams with a flick of its wrist. We came to understand it is generational, societal and individual, all at once. We also accepted that we were a long way from finding the play inside all of that. That said, I was driven to generate a piece of work that could speak to and for the Ensemble, in such a way that could communicate their ideas to the wider audience.

The creative process in theatre is exquisite because it is one of such collaboration. It is also torturous for the exact same reason. There is a terrific play by Pirandello entitled *6 Characters in Search of an Author*, the creative process of *Fearless* seriously felt much of the time like 10 actors in search of a play. We had many heated discussions about the form and structure and process of developing the script and often after these chats I would be left reeling, feeling defeated and bludgeoned or the complete opposite, feeling invigorated and inspired. We held several creative developments over the next six months, some just with members of the Ensemble, others the associate artists, and others again with everyone, depending upon the focus needed at the time. In many ways as a playwright, so much collaboration clouded the issues, at other times it revealed great truths otherwise hidden from me, so I thank the generosity and courage of all involved in the generative process.

As a playwright working out of this form of creative development, you work through so many different disciplines, it's as if we've all been happily mining clay, with everyone tossing their clay with great fervour onto the ever-increasing clay-pile. Then everyone goes away and you as the writer are left with this marvellous pile of clay that is utterly shapeless. Then begins your process of sculpting it into something else, something that has resonance and relevance to those involved in the mining process, but also something that will connect those themes to the wider audience. *Fearless* is a play that inhabits two prime central realities: the various characters real worlds, which are all in varying degrees of decay, yet they remain tenuously linked: a streetscape, a bar, a bedroom, a chair, a soup kitchen, a TV. The second reality that dominates the space is the metaphoric externalisation of the character's inner emotional and psychological worlds: The Hell Room, where the central figure of Lotte mirrors or explores or exposes these characters inner truths. It is through these antithetical realities that I hope to have captured the 'motion sickness' of the lonely experience.

As the playwright I would like to thank the relentless support of the exquisite Rashelle, for reading drafts, feeding into the themes, ideas and characters of this play as well as for putting our children to bed whilst I remained obsessively ensconced at my desk. To my dramaturg Hilary Bell for asking the right questions with her gentle smile of knowingness that always undid me and clarified the bleeding obvious that had masterfully eluded me up until that moment. And for Lucy Bell too, for helping me see there was another play emerging within the script, and for having the wisdom to get me to separate them into two plays, even though it meant her character was cut from *Fearless*. And finally to the team at Milk Crate Theatre, Maree for saying each draft was better than the last, Siena for being flexible in her thinking, Kate for pushing me to define what it was I was even writing and Beck for her wisdom in working with the Ensemble. I also feel proud by the confidence and extreme support from Carriageworks. The two Lisa's especially are a force for good (and not evil), and if you can ever harness their collective power you will the better for it.

I am nervous how such a hybrid theatrical beast will be greeted by an audience, yet I remain convinced that theatre of merit is always audacious, provocative and daring, and if it gets to speak from a place of authenticity then I say let's risk all in the pursuit of embracing the power inherent in telling our story.

Fearless was first produced by Milk Crate Theatre at Carriageworks, Sydney, on 13 September 2012, with the following cast:

MUT-DOG	Sean Barker
GIZMO	Owen Gill
DOGTAG	Michael Godlee
LOTTE	Christa Hughes
CLIPPER	Russell Kiefel
CARLOTTA	Ray Morgan
CHIKA	Wayne Schmidt
PT	John Turanga
PEPPER	Bridget Wood
CRYSTAL	Sarah Woods

Playwright / Director, Mirra Todd
Musical Director and Composer, Daryl Wallis
Lighting Designer, Ross Graham
Set and Costume Designer, Dylan Tonkin
Stage Manager, Asha Watson
Production Manager, Kate McBride

CHARACTERS

LOTTE, loneliness personified, she is centuries old; reflects the characters' inner world, to confront and challenge them, to console them, to inspire them

CHIKA, a 40-year-old who deals illicit drugs and is used to intimidating people by his size and demeanour, who finds redemption after being bashed

PT, a person who has turned to clowning to deal with his 'anger issues' since being denied ongoing access to his children after a messy divorce

PEPPER, a 60-year-old woman (a rough sleeper), had her son taken away years earlier and lost contact with him; a suicide survivor—she has deep but faded scars on her wrists

DOG-TAG, a returned soldier suffering post-traumatic stress, haunted by the images of the innocent people he has killed, this makes him vulnerable and suicidal

CARLOTTA, a 55-year-old drag queen struggling with the fact that he is no longer attractive; now housebound with agoraphobia; has joined an internet dating service, but in his imagination he is still vibrant and youthful

GIZMO, a gambling addict who finds solace and belonging at the local pub and playing the TAB

CLIPPER, a very successful businessman, who is struggling with the ongoing decay of his beloved wife who is suffering from Alzheimer's

CRYSTAL, a carpark attendant whose husband died of cancer—a widow in her third year of grieving, who has become quite bitter

MUT-DOG, a 40-year-old man, the long lost son of Pepper, suffers from Asperger's Syndrome and is genius and child in equal measure

PLAYWRIGHT'S NOTE

Fearless is set in The Hell Room, which bleeds into and out of various people's lives, and the remnants or decaying reality of their worlds. As the playwright, in creating Lotte (loneliness personified) I chose the theatrical convention of a cabaret persona, to ensure she had legitimate gravitas and mischievousness in equal measure. The tag lines could also be projected/written/embodied in a set/lighting style aligned with the production elements. There are also whispers, sounds from the shadows written in the script (*in italics*), and these are to be sounds/words coming from 'elsewhere'—however the words themselves are specific to the character uttering them. The songs are also written in italics to clarify when a character is singing.

SCRIPT FORMAT

/	denotes an overlap in either the following line and/or action by the other character
Silence	indicates an internal shift in the action
Pause	indicates an external shift in the action
Beat	indicates a moment, as marked by the character
Segue	indicates the scenes bleed slowly from one to the next (characters must not freeze)
Transition	denotes the establishment of the new scene

This play went to press before the end of rehearsals and may differ from the play as performed.

THE SONGS

The songs in the production are all original works, generated by
the Ensemble working in partnership with Daryl Wallis (composer)
Christa Hughes (singer) and Mirra Todd (playwright) in a generative
creative process.

1. The Hell Room: Words by Owen Gill,
   music by Daryl Wallis and Christa Hughes.
2. Puff Puff, words by Sarah Woods and Mirra Todd,
   music Daryl Wallis and Christa Hughes.
3. Hell Head: Words by Michael Godlee,
   music by Daryl Wallis and Christa Hughes.
4. Where did he go: Words by Michael Godlee,
   music by Daryl Wallis and Christa Hughes.
5. Can't say no to trouble: Words by John Turanga,
   music by Daryl Wallis and Christa Hughes.
6. Give me the devil: Words by Bridget Wood,
   music by Daryl Wallis and Christa Hughes.
7. P.M.A: Words by Ray Morgan,
   music by Daryl Wallis and Christa Hughes.
8. Freedom. Words by Robin Levy,
   music by Daryl Wallis and Christa Hughes.
9. Down on my knees: Words by Wayne Schmidt,
   music by Daryl Wallis and Christa Hughes.
10. Lotte's Song: Words and music by Christa Hughes.
11. Canine Best Friend: Words Sean Barker,
    music by Daryl Wallis and Sean Barker.
12. I'm doing fine: Words by Mirra Todd,
    music by Daryl Wallis and Christa Hughes.
13. Fallen Through The Crack: Words by Owen Gill,
    music by Daryl Wallis and Christa Hughes.

PROLOGUE

As the audience enter, the theatre is already populated: four people in isolation living in the smallness of their lives. DOG-TAG *is eating cereal in his chair.* CLIPPER *looking at the* Business Review *waiting for a bus.* CHIKA *is counting drugs.* MUT-DOG *is sitting on the street, muttering in agitation as he does up his bootlaces.* GIZMO *is there, reading through the form guide.*

LOTTE *is illuminated in The Hell Room.*

LOTTE: *How do you think it feels to be shunned by all and sick of your own company?*
   How do you think it feels to be invisible when you're desperate to be seen?
   When the only face that looks you in the eye is your own worn out reflection
   And she don't ever even smile at you
   Just turns away disgusted, wants no connection

   Ooooooooh, baby, something's got to give
   C'mon, c'mon, baby, I'm just trying to live

   How do you think it feels when everybody thinks you're dirty, filthy scum?
   And the few rare times that you go to speak the people turn and run
   How do you think it feels to live in the street and let's face it, who calls that living?
   To be treated like a social disease, a mortal sin that won't be forgiven

   Oooh, baby, something's got to give
   C'mon, c'mon, baby, I'm just trying to live

   Don't be so spineless
   Just give some kindness
   You think I'm cheerless
   Baby I'm fearless
   Yeah maybe I'm starving
   Starving for loving
   Don't be so cheerless
   Step up and be fearless.

Loneliness makes finger puppets of us all.

DOG-TAG: Rat-a-tat-tat.
PT: Thwack.
CRYSTAL: Puff.
PEPPER: Scratch.
CRYSTAL: Puff.
CLIPPER: Blah.
GIZMO: Ka-ching!
CARLOTTA: Ha!

Welcome into The Hell Room.

> GIZMO *is illuminated at the microphone*

GIZMO: Come on into The Hell Room,
   It's easy to enter though you may not leave too soon,
   Lights are bright in The Hell Room,
   The flashing colours belie the rising gloom,
   Bells are ringing in The Hell Room,
   Pretty soon they'll be singing a sour tune,
   Something takes you over in The Hell Room.
   Demons and entities begin to croon,
   Lost your way in The Hell Room.
   With the smell of dismay, and impending doom.

   You can shed a tear in The Hell Room.
   As desperation, regret and despair begin to loom,
   If you give your life to The Hell Room.
   It will make a sad, lonely and darkening tomb.
   When you've lost it all in The Hell Room.
   You can't get it back, and part of you remains in / the womb of...

> *Transition:* CRYSTAL *smoking a cigarette.*

CRYSTAL: Puff.

> *From the shadows we hear:*

PEPPER: Scratch.
GIZMO: Ka-ching!
PT: Thwack.
CLIPPER: Blah.

MUT-DOG: *Howls.*

CRYSTAL: It's the living that kills. Living kills you all the way to dead. Every time. No bang. No swish. Just a puff, and— My husband never smoked a day in his— My husband. The C word! It's the living that— Smoking makes me feel like I'm not alone, like the smoke somehow fills that part of me that is / dead too.

LOTTE: */ Come on into The Hell Room.*

MUT-DOG: *Howls.*

CRYSTAL: I'm here to have a smoke. Can you believe I can't smoke down there? Down there. In the pit. Full of fumes and dirt and dust and the lot and I'm not allowed to bloody smoke. Apparently the government care about my health. Don't get me started about the government and my / health.

PEPPER: Hate baked beans. Hate everything about them. The smell. The texture. Even the idea / of them.

CRYSTAL: And then I breathe it out, like it's nothing.

PEPPER: Right up there with Deb potatoes and spag bol. Diet of the destitute. Dog-food the lot if you ask me. Scratch. Scratch away at the system till you get it working / for you, scratch.

LOTTE: *Come on into The Hell Room.*

GIZMO: It's good to have something, even if it can't hug you back. Even if it can't keep you warm. Waiting for *me*. For me to get a beer, pull up my stool, and there's nowhere else I can do that.

LOTTE: */ Come on into The Hell Room.*

GIZMO: Just turn up and be welcomed like / that, just welcomed.

CHIKA: I have MDMA, Angel Dust, Poppers, Snappers, Rock, Benzos, Cue Tips, Mud, Ritalin, Valium / Mesc/ aline, what's your poison?

LOTTE: *Come on into The Hell Room.*

> *The street.*

> MUT-DOG *sitting, rifling through an old, faded bag. He sees something just offstage.*

MUT-DOG: Come here, dog. Do you wanna come closer? Cuggle me? Trust me? It's late, isn't it? You're out late. So late it's almost early. For me, almost early. Maybe not so for you, dog. Lonely dog. Maybe in dog time *late* lasts seven years divided, eh? Three hundred and sixty-five days in a human year divide by seven dog days in dog years is [*in his head*] 52.142—eh? 52.142857 divide in twos equals—26.071429, which makes, let me count it out, count it out—

He does so in his head and on his fingers. Others from the shadows:

CRYSTAL: *Puff.*
PEPPER: *Scratch.*
CRYSTAL: *Puff.*
GIZMO: *Ka-ching!*
CLIPPER: *Blah.*
MUT-DOG: Night is what? One third of the daytime, despite what people babble about, so divide by thirdsies and we have—? So, your night-time may last 8,690 days, which means you are either streets ahead of me or way behind me or *even-stevens*, but *either or* maybe sit here? By me? Lie here, yes? Next to me. I won't bite.
DOG-TAG: *Rat-a-tat-tat.*
PT: *Thwack.*
CRYSTAL: *Puff.*
PEPPER: *Scratch.*
CRYSTAL: *Puff.*
CLIPPER: *Blah.*
GIZMO: *Ka-ching!*
CARLOTTA: *Ha!*

SCENE ONE

Transition: The public bar at the Century Hotel.

CLIPPER *and* GIZMO *are at the bar.* CLIPPER *is drinking,* GIZMO *is checking out the form guide. They are friendly strangers, who only know about the other that which has been revealed.*

CLIPPER: I don't suffer fools. And you, Gizmo, are one damned fool headin' straight to hell / in a—
GIZMO: Nah, see most people don't play the odds.
CLIPPER: I'm a straight talker and I'm telling you— Listen, I could take your money and double it, quadruple it—but that would just bore the shit out of you, wouldn't it? Because it's not about the money / for you.

GIZMO: It's about the game. The playing.

CLIPPER: Money's what gives me a hard-on. Cold, hard cash. Stock market, now there's a game worthy of men. A game for / the adults.

GIZMO: True for you, maybe, but it depends on your poison, for me it was always blackjack.

CLIPPER: People used to call this place The Lucky Country, but she's a toothless bitch who's lost her grip, if you ask me. People like you don't stand a chance. Not anymore.

GIZMO: Ease up there, Clipper. If I didn't get caught counting cards I'd be sitting pretty / flush.

CLIPPER: You're delusional. All gamblers are.

Segue: Dog-Tag's home.

DOG-TAG's *hibernating in his chair, eating cereal.* LOTTE *enters.*

LOTTE: Trying to punch out a couple of zeds, baby?

DOG-TAG *stands up, trying to quiet the thoughts in his mind.*

But why? It's a beautiful morning. Face the day, soldier.

DOG-TAG *is clearly distressed.*

Maybe some carbs. Have a bat, / then—

DOG-TAG *is muttering to himself, trying to exorcise his inner demons.*

Your eating irons are putrid, soldier.

DOG-TAG *takes his spoon and cleans it on his shirt.*

Segue: The hotel.

CLIPPER: Just confess, there's no strategy to poker machines.

GIZMO: So I like the pretty lights.

Segue: Dog-Tag's Home.

LOTTE: It's a beautiful morning.

Segue: The bar.

GIZMO: Speaking of, did you see the ambulances and cop cars a couple of nights ago swarm down Kingston Terrace?

CLIPPER: No, but I heard. He was always a misery, that one. Walked around like he was carrying the weight of Mount Vesuvius on his shoulders just as it was about to erupt. We've all got our pits of despair buried deep inside us, but you push down, you get on, you don't let the bastards win.

> *Beat.*

I invited him for a drink once, started babbling about blood bubbling in his chest. Scared me fucking senseless to / tell the truth.

GIZMO: Yeah, he was, I don't know—

CLIPPER: Never a smile or handshake. Drank only soft drink, for fuck's sake. Who comes to a pub and drinks soft drink? He was a child!

> *Segue: Dog-Tag's Home.*

> DOG-TAG *curls within its folds, seeking solace.*

LOTTE: Oh, you've really cracked the sads, haven't you, soldier? Well—

> LOTTE *laughs.*

> *Segue: The hotel.*

CLIPPER: You'd expect more from an ex-military.

GIZMO: Yeah, Afghanistan and Iraq before— Back in the day he was a muso.

CLIPPER: Yeah, not a musician, he was what, a drummer in the '90s / I heard.

GIZMO: Yeah, something, was someone once.

CLIPPER: An ape banging sticks at some animal hide.

> *Segue: The chair.*

> DOG-TAG *is again eating his cereal hoping to fatigue his body.*

LOTTE: Drink some concrete and harden the fuck up!

> DOG-TAG *is clearly distressed. / The poker machine's light goes crazy and /* GIZMO *is in ecstasy, a reverie.* CHIKA *is revealed on his knees in a drug-induced reverie /* DOG-TAG *shudders. He stands up; he opens an old tin that is resting on the table, rifles through until he pulls out an old faded photo of a young boy (circa 1960) and reflects on his past.*

> *It is, it is, it is, it is, it is, it is a beauuuuuuuuuuuuuuuuuutiful morning.*

> *Segue: The hotel.*

GIZMO: C'mon, number three! C'mon, you useless sack of hair! Damn!

CLIPPER takes a drink. His glass is empty, just like him. He has a moment of reflection.

Sorry, just blew my wad. What were / we—?

CLIPPER: The dead soldier. If he had have just cracked a grin he'd still be alive. Maybe taught self-defence for kids at the local gym. Had a fucking purpose.

GIZMO: Heard he put a barrel in his mouth and blew out his / brains.

CLIPPER: Now that is a stand-out act of cowardice.

Segue: Dog-Tag's home.

DOG-TAG regards the photo.

DOG-TAG: Where did he go, that fresh-faced kid in / the family album?

LOTTE: Just dig into your tucker there. You have become a complete *wombat*. Waste-of-military-budget-and-time. Keep pouring food into your shit locker, punch out some zeds, and maybe you'll forget how many people you killed. Rat-a-tat-tat!

DOG-TAG stows the photo away dutifully, and starts counting out in his head and on his fingers, remembering all his victims. He is muttering to himself as he does this. LOTTE begins making DOG-TAG some more cereal as he counts out the number of the dead in his head.

DOG-TAG: Solomon Islands, Operation Anode, thirty-four targeted enemy KIA.

LOTTE: *Thirty-four, baby.*

DOG-TAG: Iraq, Operation Kruger, thirty-three dead. East Timor, / Operation Astute, seventeen civilians dead and—

LOTTE: *Thirty-three, baby.*

DOG-TAG: —one friendly fire. East Peace Process, Operation Paladin, twelve women and children equals, how many? How many? How—?

LOTTE: Rat-a-tat-tat, baby. Seventeen women, children and babies, baby.

LOTTE hands DOG-TAG the bowl. He takes it and eats voraciously, hoping to calm his mind.

Tani, that was his name, twelve years old. And Abdiel, four years old. Jaweed, his name meant 'Timeless', 'Eternal'. Ha, just seven years old. Amina, means 'The Peaceful One'—not so peaceful now is she, hey Dog-Tag? Rat-a-tat-tat—

LOTTE: *They are all gone. Gone. Those children. Gone.*

> *Segue: The hotel.*

CLIPPER: Used to sit at the corner table over there, always kept / to himself.
GIZMO: Yeah, don't trust people who keep / to themselves.
CLIPPER: Why didn't he grow a pair? Reminds me of my middle boy, still waiting for his to drop.
GIZMO: We've all got our own shit / to peddle, you know?
CLIPPER: They all blame their daddy in the end, chicken shits!
GIZMO: Not much to / do.
CLIPPER: None of our beeswax.

> *Segue: Dog-Tag's Home.*

> DOG-TAG *is looking out, defeated.*

LOTTE: Punch those zeds, baby. Hey, let's sing a lullaby, you and me. Let's sings ourselves to sleep. Just you and me, baby. Together.

> DOG-TAG *starts to sings.* LOTTE *joins him.*

DOG-TAG: *Where, where did he go, that fresh-faced kid in the family album?*
Where, where did he go, where did he go?
All gone wrong. All gone. Gone.

> DOG-TAG *is asleep, but not peacefully.*

LOTTE: Tomorrow will be a better day. Tomorrow will be a beautiful morning.

> LOTTE *kisses his forehead then slowly leaves.*

> *Segue:* PT *is warming up before his performance. He draws a chalk circle, then starts pulling lots of different funny faces and gestures in an invisible mirror.*

> *Segue: The hotel.*

GIZMO: Want a tip on race four?
CLIPPER: Mate, there are better ways to lose your money. Hey, Mike, another double scotch, no ice, cheers!

> *Segue: The street.*

> PT, *starts to juggle, badly.*

Do you play the market? It's not gambling, it's mathematics.
GIZMO: So is counting cards!

    Segue: The street.

    PEPPER *arrives and watches* PT *for a moment.*

    Segue: The bar.

CLIPPER: I got some insider trading. Don't say you heard it from me.
GIZMO: They'll have to beat it out / of me.

SCENE TWO

Transition: The street.

PT *is trying to master the craft of juggling with inconsistent results. A decision is made by* PEPPER *to connect with a stranger. The stranger is less interested.*

Loneliness is a child with an ant farm.

PEPPER: It's a beautiful morning.
PT: Yeah, beautiful.
PEPPER: I love days like today, don't you?
PT: Any day when you're not six feet under is a good day, I always / say.
PEPPER: It's good to be alive.
PT: Living the good life.
PEPPER: In The Lucky Country.
PT: Doesn't get much better than this.
PEPPER: No, this is as good as it gets.
PT: Who could ask for more?
PEPPER: Not me, that's / for sure.
PT: No, count your blessing, I / always say.
PEPPER: Just the one?

    From the shadows:

DOG-TAG: *Peace.*
MUT-DOG: *Remembering.*
GIZMO: *Happiness.*

    Transition: The street.

PEPPER: So, how are you?

PT: Can't complain.

PEPPER: That's lovely.

PT: Lovely?

PEPPER: That you don't feel the need to bitch and moan like / so many others.

PT: Oh, no, sorry, you misunderstand, I *can't* complain. Literally. It's a court order. I have anger management issues.

From the shadows:

CRYSTAL: *Don't get me started.*

CLIPPER: *We've all got our pits of despair.*

CRYSTAL: *Don't get me started.*

PT: The judge thought sending me to clown school would be the answer to all my woes.

LOTTE *laughs from the shadows.*

PEPPER: Anger issues?

PT: Messy divorce.

From the shadows:

CARLOTTA: *Positive Mental Attitude.*

PT: The ex painted a pretty bad picture; see, I have mental health issues.

PEPPER: Mental health / issues?

PT: ADHD. BHP. A touch of / ACDC.

PEPPER: We all have our crosses to / bear.

PT: And addiction issues.

PEPPER: Well, that which does not kill us, you know!

PT: So I like a drink or twenty.

PEPPER: We all need to unwind somehow, am I right?

PT: My wife wanted to take the kids back to Perth after the divorce, and the judge said yes, because of all my / issues.

PEPPER: Issues.

They laugh awkwardly because they are embarrassed and feel exposed. They recover.

PT: I smashed his car with a crowbar.

PEPPER: Probably had it coming.

PT: You're a decent sort.

PEPPER: Oh, not according to the judge.

PT: Judge?

PEPPER: Took my son away from me.
PT: Justice doesn't equal fairness, am I right?
PEPPER: I have issues too.

> *From the shadows:*

GIZMO: *Hope.*
CLIPPER: *Laughter.*
CRYSTAL: *Love.*
DOG-TAG: *Memories.*
PT: Well, you are human.
PEPPER: Let's just say misery loves company.
PT: Nice to meet you, *misery.*

> *Segue:* LOTTE *is illuminated in The Hell Room.* PT, *and* PEPPER *laugh—it is slightly forced. They laugh a little too long, until it quickly exhausts itself and they stare out, both miserable.* LOTTE *mocks them.* PT *confesses something.*

Truth is, I spend most of the day sitting in my tiny flat, watching children's television shows and just— I woke up this morning and I can't remember when or how I even got— How did I—?

LOTTE: *I woke up this morning*
And I can't remember when,
Or how I even got here,
In this cold and lonely den,

And now when I think back on it,
My life was always 'bout to blow,
I can't keep away or say no,
To trouble...
Say no, no, no, no, no.

Morning rain keeps on falling,
Like the tears that fall from my eyes,
I can't help, I just can't help thinking
There was a time the sun, it used to shine,

So now when I think back on it,
My life was always 'bout to blow,
I can't keep away or say 'no' to trouble
Say no, no, no, no, no.

The Hell Room disappears.

PEPPER: Kids get stolen all the time. Stolen while you sleep. Stolen while you shop. Stolen while you cook them their dinner. Just stolen.

PT: You don't *have* to be black. But it doesn't help if—

Segue: Carlotta's bedroom.

CARLOTTA *is alone, wearing only a slip, a padded bra underneath, in front of her full-length mirror, curled, vulnerable, feeling judged by her own reflection. Her face is fully made-up, in drag, but she is completely bald. She looks deeply at her own visage and feels it doesn't reflect her anymore.*

CARLOTTA: Mirror, mirror, on the wall, wouldn't you like the sweetest fuck of all? I'm six feet of man-flesh just wasting away, yearning for some hot thing to bring the batteries and plug us both in.

Her hand touches her reflection, looking for a moment of touch, of connection, but it isn't there. Her sadness is leaking through, she tries to cover.

Segue: The street.

They have found their rage at life's injustice.

PT: Stolen by a court order that tells me *don't worry, be happy*. Paint a smile on my face and be / grateful.

PEPPER: There's no word for people like us, parents who've lost their / children.

PT: No-one's ever cared enough to give us a name, that's why.

Loneliness makes you feel like the fat, ugly girl at the ball.

Segue: Carlotta's bedroom.

CARLOTTA *looks over her shoulder to the audience, exposed. She shies away from their gaze, and her own exposure.*

CARLOTTA: Sun's nearly up. Honey, you should only be seen with back lighting. Look at yourself, seriously.

She stands, awkward and exposed. As she does, from The Hell Room we hear LOTTE *sing.*

LOTTE: *For love and fuck and / hope.*

Segue: The street.

PEPPER: We've all made mistakes.

PT: I make the same ones, again / and again, and again, and—

SCENE THREE

Transition: Carlotta's bedroom.

CARLOTTA, *now in front of the mirror in the slip, is checking her face make-up, she is embarrassed.* LOTTE *enters the bedroom.* CARLOTTA *looks in the mirror.*

CARLOTTA: Six foot and bulletproof! Ha!

> LOTTE *sings.*

LOTTE: Positive mental attitude, that keeps your hope alive.

> CARLOTTA *looks in the mirror, puts on her wig.* LOTTE *laughs as* CARLOTTA *turns away from the mirror. She sets up a camcorder, and sits in front of it. She is exposed.*

CARLOTTA: Okay Here goes. My name is… My name is… Fuck, to forget a name. Start again. My stage name was Hedda Cabbage. Ha!

> *She grabs a kimono from behind the mirror, dresses herself, then moves to the camera and re-sets it.* LOTTE *picks up the camera.*

LOTTE: Ready for your close-up?

> LOTTE *focuses on* CARLOTTA. *She is exposed, vulnerable.*

CARLOTTA: Surprising that a Glamour like me would need to— Not that I'm bitter. Far from it, sweet-cheek, I was bitter before. The guttersnipes you see on stage now, they are not drag queens, honey, they are west-side street whores that are picked up from truckstops. It's all about super-trash Tuesday. But yes, I do like trash. When God sends you lemons, I always say made lemonade, stick some vodka in it and you're good to go. Ha!

> *She fractures, her faced is breaking. She is angry and exposed.*

This sucks big, donkey-dick.

> *Silence.* CARLOTTA *accepts her vulnerability, and decides to expose it on camera in the hope of discovering… love. There is a real element of emotional bravery revealed.*

Now, why am I doing this, you must be asking? But you should know that answer yourself. I'm fifty-five and it just feels time before I'm left on the…

LOTTE *sings.*

LOTTE: *You have your PMA to keep your life alive.*

CARLOTTA *feeling pain, but subtle and sublime.*

CARLOTTA: I like footy. I like V8s.

She softens, yet is becoming defiant in her presentation online, which will ultimately be her undoing.

I don't like racists. Or bullies. Or those people that check in the grocery aisle for twelve items or less, when they have a cart full with crap for a family of five. The suburban tit-less I call them. Don't they get it? That aisle is for people like— That aisle is for people like—

She touches her face in the mirror.

What / the fuck?

LOTTE *sings.*

LOTTE: *You question 'what the fuck?' This fucking PMA.*

CARLOTTA *takes off her kimono. It drops to the ground.*

CARLOTTA: This is me. If you like what you see—call.

LOTTE *turns off the camera, places it back in front of* CARLOTTA. *She slowly moves to her and leans over her shoulder.*

Segue: CRYSTAL *is illuminated in her lounge room, flicking TV channels.*

CRYSTAL: Reality looks much better when it's produced for the masses. For me *reality* is, well—

She turns off the remote.

Segue: Carlotta's bedroom.

LOTTE *and* CARLOTTA *whispers in unison.*

LOTTE & CARLOTTA: For fuck and love and hope.

LOTTE *squeezes* CARLOTTA's *shoulder then exits.*

When push comes, loneliness shoves.

SCENE FOUR

Transition: Crystal's lounge room.

CRYSTAL *is cold, physically and emotionally, and yet her love for Des burns like a furnace.*

CRYSTAL: Used to be you with the remote. Bloody flick, flick, flick, did my head in, but now— Look what you've reduced me to. I'll be getting cats next. Except I've read in the *Weekly* how cats like to snuggle up on a person's bed while they're sleeping. What's that about? Besides, I couldn't stand havin' anything that wasn't you laying there next to—

> *She stands, and falls into her husband's cardigan and feels loved. Reality strikes.*

Still haven't heard a word from your ratty sister. Not since we put you six feet under. Over two years! Christ, that one can hold a grudge. I told her she wasn't getting her hands on your mother's good crystal set till I was lying right there next to you, which apparently she indicated may take too long. Seemed to think I had no right to it. Like I wasn't family. I said to her, I said, 'Lorna, after thirty-four years of marriage, if I'm not family then I no longer have to put up with your blasted whingeing, but am and so I do have to put up with—' Anyway, that shut her trap!

> *Silence. She is aware she is alone.*

Weather's been crap.

> *From the shadows:*

DOG-TAG: *Rat-a-tat-tat.*
PT: *Thwack.*
PEPPER: *Scratch.*
CLIPPER: *Blah.*
GIZMO: *Ka-ching!*
CARLOTTA: *Ha!*

> CRYSTAL *lights a cigarette. Makes a decision.*

CRYSTAL: So here it— I think I've decided I don't believe in God. Sorry if that's a shocker, but I just— It doesn't feel true anymore, you know. To me. And before you start in, 'no, it's not about you going off and dying on me that turned me heart to stone'. Me heart isn't stone, just heavy, like it's full of little rocks or pebbles or bits of debris. Yeah, that's it, full of bits of debris. But no, it's not that. I just— I've been thinking that God, you know the idea of God, well— I've been thinking that God is just something us wet saps made up, trying to pretend that we aren't all alone. But the truth is, well—

She confesses.

With you I never felt, but without you—

Segue: The street.

MUT-DOG *pulls a pizza box out of his bag. He opens it and pulls out a slice.*

MUT-DOG: Mmmm. Meatlovers.

Segue: The lounge room.

CRYSTAL: Anyway, love, I'm knackered. I'm off to bed.

She begins to take off the cardigan.

It smells of me now. Just of me.

SCENE FIVE

Transition: The street.

MUT-DOG *eating a slice. He is blissful.*

MUT-DOG: Hey, dog, I see you there. Want some meatlovers pizza? It's pretty fresh, not that you care, you lick your own arse. Don't scare off. Maybe just watch me from there for now.

He sits and eats his slice as he talks.

Thanks for coming back. Was just trickin' with my snarls and growls. Good at make-believe, since from before the *taking*. The *she* that sang to me and made all the hurty-hurts become bubbles float high up into the magic faraway sky. Do you have a family? A *family*, dog? I don't.

Beat.

Will you feel safe if I hold you on my lap? Even if I cry? You can lick away my tears. It feels good when you lick me like all the good feelings have fallen back from the sky and slam-dunked into my eyes and are spilling out again. Makes me queasy and wheezy and blissful together. Has much happened to you? Have you hurt things? Killed things? I can keep your secrets.

CHIKA *enters the street, obviously on drugs. The Hell Room alights.*

CHIKA: Hey, man, you got pizza! Can I—?

MUT-DOG: Shhh. Quiet, you fool.

CHIKA: Hey, brother, you want an *E*?

MUT-DOG: You'll frighten him off. / Here, boy!

CHIKA: I tell you, bro, this stuff is like dizzy dancing; like every fairy tale is real. Man, I love this fucking / feeling; drugs are the—

MUT-DOG: Here, boy? Where are you, in the shadows?

CHIKA: Drugs are the best, am I right? I'm right. An *E* for a slice, / great deal.

MUT-DOG: You in the darkness? In the secret / places?

CHIKA: Come out, come out, wherever you are. / It's time to party.

MUT-DOG: *I'm talking to my friend!*

CHIKA: I can be your friend, I can be a very friendly fella, so don't fuck me off. I've got pills, c'mon, we can party. Come on, bro, how / 'bout that slice, eh?

MUT-DOG: You stop talking. You swine. Why do you / even exist?

CHIKA: All I'm after is a feed, where is the fucking / harm in that?

MUT-DOG: Leave us alone.

CHIKA: Who the fuck is *us*? You / like royalty?

MUT-DOG: I said leave!

CHIKA: Watch your mouth, boy.

MUT-DOG: I'm not a little boy dreaming / no more no more no—

CHIKA: You don't want to get on the wrong / side of me, trust me.

MUT-DOG: When I was a boy I did jump from the wrong side / of the bed.

CHIKA: I was in an excellent buzz-mood, but you're fucking inhospitality / yanked it.

MUT-DOG: I flew. Second day, more scaring; but little-boy daring; I jumped from the tabletop. Landed all *ouch* but see how big boy / I am with not crying.

CHIKA: I don't like to be yanked. Is this / getting through that thick skull?

MUT-DOG: Now more daring, still playing at flying. To let the wind carry me up all 'Icarus' and 'not too close to the sun' flying. But like 'Icarus' I / need wings that don't melt.

CHIKA: Stop your gibberish and pay me some fucking respect!

> MUT-DOG *slowly stands, and looks directly at* CHIKA, *who is thrown by being blatantly ignored.* MUT-DOG *has decided to end the conversation without malice but with violence.*

MUT-DOG: I don't feel things, you know.
CHIKA: You don't—? / What?
MUT-DOG: Nothing.
CHIKA: / What?
MUT-DOG: I don't feel things.
CHIKA: What? Don't feel—?

> MUT-DOG *releases a primal scream; then proceeds to violently beat* CHIKA, *who is taken unaware.*

> *Segue: The bar.*

> CLIPPER *and* GIZMO *are at the bar.* DOG-TAG *is, alone.*

GIZMO: Twenty-eight quid right here!
CLIPPER: You gonna let me invest it and quadruple your—?
GIZMO: What do ya reckon?
CLIPPER: Another act of cowardice.

> *Segue: The street.*

> MUT-DOG *is standing above a bloodied* CHIKA. *He has the pizza in his hand, he sits down and begins eating it.*

MUT-DOG: You frightened off my friend.

> LOTTE *is illuminated in The Hell Room.*

LOTTE: Your spills turned to pills,
   The grass grew into weed,

> LOTTE *moves to* CHIKA *and picks him up. She wipes the blood from his face—maternal and lover in equal measure. She walks him into The Hell Room.*

Chika tells it like it is.
CHIKA: My spills turned to pills,
   The grass grew into weed,
   All the love that I been given,
   Became a desperate plead.

'Cause I'm good as a front,
And can smoke up a blunt,
But when I'm down,
I'm down on my knees.
All this shit, on the street,
It just fell at my feet,
It was then that I sold,
My soul to the hole,
And now find myself,
Completely out in to cold.

> *Transition: The Century Hotel, public bar.*

> CLIPPER *and* GIZMO *are at the bar.* DOG-TAG *alone.* LOTTE *begins to bandage* CHIKA's *wounds.*

CLIPPER: So, straight back to the pokies, with the pretty fucking lights?

GIZMO: It's good to have a hobby!

CLIPPER: No. A hobby is paying $300 for some whore to do what your wife won't, and I'm not talking vacuuming your scrotum, I'm talking about the *bring on the stroke* stuff. At my age it's good to have the *'bring on the stoke stuff'* locked down.

GIZMO: Sure, yes, right, okay fine, but for me—

Loneliness rolls the loaded dice.

GIZMO: For me it's good to have something, even if it can't hug you back. Even if it can't keep you warm. It's good to have something that is always there. Sometimes your mate, when it throws you a win. Sometimes a mug, when it don't. But you know what? It's some *where* to be. It's some *thing* to do. And it's always there. Right there. Waiting for me. Waiting for *me*. For me to get a beer, pull up my stool and there's nowhere else I can do that. Just turn up, and be welcomed like that. Nowhere. / Just turn up and be welcomed like that.

> *The Hell Room is illuminated.*

LOTTE: Money!

GIZMO: That's how a man knows he's got significance, Clipper. Having a place that welcomes you. It's not the money.

LOTTE: Money!

CLIPPER: But I never see you leave, it's almost like you / live here.

GIZMO: It's the company; it's the friendship; it's the—

LOTTE: Money!

GIZMO: The belonging.

LOTTE: *Come on into The Hell Room,*
It's easy to enter though you may not leave too soon,
Lights are bright in The Hell Room,
The flashing colours belie the rising gloom,
Bells are ringing in The Hell Room,
Pretty soon they'll be singing a sour tune,
Lost your way in The Hell Room.
With the smell of loss, and feeling of impending doom.
You can shed a tear in The Hell Room.

GIZMO: I thought this time, I'd be a winner.

> *All the others laugh brutally, mocking him. They toss money at him from the shadows, he reacts as if being beaten by each note.*

> GIZMO *shamelessly picks up the money.*

I won't give them the satisfaction of stopping. I'm no quitter.

> LOTTE *laughs.*

> *Segue: The street.*

> CRYSTAL *lights a cigarette.*

> *From the shadows, we hear actors whisper in a round throughout the song:*

VOICES FROM SHADOWS: Look. Look at his face. His face. Please. He's only four. A baby. Please. Please, look at his face. Look, look at his—

LOTTE: *Fallen through the crack,*
There is no turning back,
Day turns into night,
Grey turns into black.

Loneliness plays with the meat.

SCENE SIX

Transition: The street.

PEPPER *is wandering past when* CRYSTAL *draws her in.*

CRYSTAL: Eight nearly.

PEPPER: What are you rabbiting on about?

CRYSTAL: She started early today!

PEPPER: Have a heart, Crystal. She's been trawling these streets looking for her kid for years and years, and everyone has given up, her husband, the cops. It's not right. It's not fair what happens / to a mother when her—

> *Actors whisper from the shadows.*

SHADOWS: Look. Look at his face. His face. Please. He's only four— A baby. Please. Please, look at his face. Look, look at his—

CRYSTAL: Still handing out that photo of him, and it's been four years. Four! That photo is not him, not anymore, just confuses— I keep / telling her.

PEPPER: It's the last photo of him she took, you know that, / you're just being a—

CRYSTAL: How in the hell is anyone going to know that he's eight / unless I tell them?

PEPPER: Show some compassion, / Jesus, Crystal!

CRYSTAL: He's another boy / now.

PEPPER: She's not imagining him. She had a son. Christ, she / has a son.

CRYSTAL: Yeah, well maybe, shit happens. But I don't litter the street with my dirty laundry!

> PEPPER *slaps* CRYSTAL, *hard. Both are in shock, neither actually can grasp how what happened just happened.*

PEPPER: I'm—? I'm—? I'm—?

CRYSTAL: You slapped me.

PEPPER: I've never hit anyone before. In my life.

CRYSTAL: I'd say you're a natural.

> *She is suddenly is very emotional.* PEPPER *is awkward, doesn't know what to do. She partly wants to hug* CRYSTAL *to reassure her and partly wants to slap her again, very conflicted.* CRYSTAL *is revealed and can't hide it, even from herself.*

Sorry. Must be shock. Delayed reaction. Why did you hit me?

PEPPER: You know nothing about it. Being a mother.

CRYSTAL: Why did you hit me?

> LOTTE *enters.* CRYSTAL *remains in shock.*

> LOTTE *remains invisible to* CRYSTAL *during the following:*

LOTTE: It's a beautiful morning.

> PEPPER *stares directly at* LOTTE.

PEPPER: You can bugger off, I'm not in the mood for your shit / today.

LOTTE: It's a / beauti—

PEPPER: I won't warn you again, you— We are fallible, sure, as people we—? But that doesn't— I will not go quietly into the—

> LOTTE *sizes her up for a moment, and then hisses at her, as though recognising a nemesis.*

Over my dead body.

> LOTTE *leaves, but laughs as she has also found her way back in to* PEPPER.

CRYSTAL: It's because I'm a horrible human being, that's why, isn't it? Why you hit me?

PEPPER: I made a mistake.

CRYSTAL: I never had kids, I was barren. Nothing to be done about it. So I got on with it. Why can't people just get on, you know? Just get on.

> *Beat.*

Always thought I'd slug right back.

> *Beat.*

Saw myself as this rock that couldn't break, no matter what, and then— Then you go and I— I—? I—?

PEPPER: I make lots of mistakes. I'm so— I'm sorry. I make mistakes. I lost my boy years and years ago, you touched a nerve. That's all. Touched a nerve. It wasn't you. It was—

> LOTTE *is illuminated at The Hell Room.* PEPPER *looks to* LOTTE, *they connect through a shared secret.* LOTTE *sings.*

LOTTE: *Home is where the heart is,*
That's what I always—

CRYSTAL *stands.*

CRYSTAL: Better get back to it, I guess.
PEPPER: Sorry? Yes, sure. Sorry, I didn't—
CRYSTAL: Next time, Pepper, *pow*, right in the kisser!

> *They laugh, but it seeps out from a place of shame.* CRYSTAL *bristles.*

You're a / natural.

> CRYSTAL *exits.* LOTTE *takes over a bottle of chardonnay, and takes out the cork, takes a swig and then hands it to* PEPPER, *who also takes a drink.*

PEPPER: You. Why do you—? Why me?
LOTTE: You know why.
PEPPER: Yes. Yes I—
LOTTE: *Home is where the heart is.*
PEPPER: That's what I always—
LOTTE: *I feel rusty and it's your birthday.*
BOTH: So here's to you with a chardonnay.

> LOTTE *returns to The Hell Room,* PEPPER *is drinking and remembering. She slowly disintegrates into her grief and shame during the song.*

LOTTE: *My brown-eyed boy was taken away,*
   But in my heart he's here to stay.
   It left a wound that never heals,
   I'll never get used to how it feels.
   Fuck God, give me the Devil
   I can talk to him on his level.

   My favourite niece lives on a farm,
   She's his age and loves a yarn,
   I'd visit but I haven't a clue,
   What to talk about, to be true blue.

   They say I mustn't grumble,
   God will catch me if I tumble,
   And everything will be alright
   As long as I fight the good fight.

Fuck God, give me the Devil
I can talk to him on his level.
I can talk to him on his level
I can talk, I can talk, I can talk
To him on his level.

Fuck God, give me the Devil
I can talk to him on his level.

Home is where the heart is,
That's what I always say.

> *Segue: The bar.*

> CLIPPER *takes a drink.* GIZMO *is studying his form guide.* DOG-TAG *enters with a soft drink, and sits in his chair. They regard each other. Silence.*

> *Segue: The street.*

> PEPPER *harnesses her rage.*

PEPPER: Fuck God, give me the Devil.
LOTTE: That's why, honey.

> *Lights in The Hell Room go out.*

Loneliness adds a side order of fries.

SCENE SEVEN

Transition: The bar.

CLIPPER *skulls his scotch.* GIZMO *sitting there figuring out the odds.* DOG-TAG *stewing silently.*

CLIPPER: Hey, barkeep, a round on me for Gizmo and— A round all round. Round and round the—

> PT *enters in his clown make-up, as* CLIPPER *grabs a bottle of scotch and an extra glass.* PT *sits.*

Wow, is the circus in town?
PT: Don't.
CLIPPER: Fine, it's a celebration. On me. Fuck, we can't have a sad clown.
PT: Fucking don't.

GIZMO: I swear, Clipper, you could upset a bride on her wedding day just by / turning up.

CLIPPER: Everyone is a bloody misery guts these days. A pack of ratbags.

GIZMO: Only if you're dealing the deck.

CLIPPER *pours two scotches and hands one to* PT.

CLIPPER: Here, make yourself more agreeable.

PT: I shouldn't.

CLIPPER: Fuck the shouldn'ts! Gizmo?

GIZMO: As I always say, none of this and none of that, but plenty of the other.

He takes PT*'s drink.* CLIPPER *pours another for* PT. *Hands it to him, but* PT *hesitates.*

CLIPPER: This bitch of a country is getting more of a nanny state every bleeding day. Everyone's a bunch of wowsers, if you ask me. I'll tell you something for nothing, time was people had each other's back, but now, these days it's every man for his / fucking self.

MUT-DOG *enters like an alien, oblivious to the others. Everyone looks at him, slightly confronted. He sits, and then slowly drinks in the others. He looks to* PT

MUT-DOG: I like your clothes.

PT: Thanks.

MUT-DOG: You got a really big heart.

PT *smiles.*

PT: Yeah. My kids used to always / say that.

MUT-DOG: Kids are the / best.

PT: / Best.

CLIPPER: / I was talking here. You don't just interrupt a / person's conversation.

MUT-DOG: Here has the heat pumping, keeps me all roasty warm.

PT: Yes. Yes, warm. My flat is so—

From the shadows:

PEPPER: So, so, so—

CRYSTAL: Cold.

PEPPER: So cold.

Segue: The bar.

MUT-DOG: Did you hear? Lost *Navvy Joe* this week, probably pneumonia. Let's all bow our heads. The cold and the—

CLIPPER: Who? / What?

MUT-DOG: *Navvy Joe*, that's our name for him, but still—

PT: Lost? You mean—?

MUT-DOG: Like a doornail.

PT: I don't know any—

MUT-DOG: You were there. I saw you draw your circle to keep us out.

PT: You blaming me? I didn't— Me—? Why not, of course, trouble always—

> PT *takes the glass of scotch and takes a drink. An ambulance siren is heard, close by, but moving away.*

MUT-DOG: Saw the Rambo ambos tuck him into their plastic sheet and shove him all cold and still onto their metal stretcher. They'll hold their own wakey-wake for *Navvy Joe* even though they don't even know his name. They'll toast to him, at the end of their shift, because they know one thing, you Mr *buy-'em-a-drink* don't want to admit.

CLIPPER: What's that my intrepid / friend?

MUT-DOG: It's more than we'll do.

> *Silence.*

CLIPPER: This is exactly what I was getting at, nowadays it's every man for him / self.

MUT-DOG: / That's a porky pie.

CLIPPER: I beg yours?

MUT-DOG: We're a pack animal. Like dogs. We / belong in packs.

CLIPPER: Did you say we're / dogs!

MUT-DOG: The other yesterday, I saw the lights change at the intersection. One woman, it caught her peripheral, she misread the signal. She starts walking. Step, step, step, step. One in, all in, clippity-clop go the hooves of all the cattle. There would have been fifteen, twenty people all halfway across the road, blindly following. When the cars that had right of way started honking and screaming their *'you fucking morons'* abuse and trying to drive through the crowd the people were in shock. Colour them surprised, some kept walking, others stopped dead. Immobilised. The ones that made it worse were the ones that started heading back to the curb, dumb head of cattle the lot. Clippity-clop. Complete pandemonium, ma nama num.

> MUT-DOG *jumps high in the air, then chases his own tail.*

PT: Down, boy.

MUT-DOG: Dogs have more / sense.

PT: / I miss my boy.

CLIPPER: You're right! Entire basis of the stock market, establishing trends for people to blindly— Enough of that. Do you invest?

> *Beat.*

Unlikely. Sorry. How about a drink? For this Navvy Joe fella.

MUT-DOG: Is it a party? For Navvy Joe?

CLIPPER: Sure. Why the fuck not? We got the clown here and / everything

PT: I said don't.

MUT-DOG: I've never been to a party.

CLIPPER: Bull-fucking-shit.

MUT-DOG: Why do you swear, all black words with no colour inside?

CLIPPER: Good question, good fucking question.

> *He laughs at his own joke. Calls out to* DOG-TAG, *who is stewing in his own juices.*

Hey, miseryguts, do you want to join us for a party for—? Hey, what's your name, boy?

MUT-DOG: Mut-Dog.

CLIPPER: For Mut—?

> *Beat.*

For Mut-Dog's friend Navvy Joe, a little celebration, lest we forget, right, soldier?

> DOG-TAG *remains sitting, motionless.*

Your loss. Bar keep, let's have a party, drinks for all my / newly minted friends. For a fallen veteran.

> DOG-TAG *slowly stands and moves to* CLIPPER—*it is a face-off.*
> DOG-TAG *wants to kill someone.*

DOG-TAG: One more word and I will end you.

Silence. CLIPPER *is feeling very threatened, he becomes a frightened child.*

MUT-DOG: Bubble-wrap it if you / must.

PT *stands, he is furious. He skulls his drink, pours himself another. He is standing there, everyone watching him. He takes the drink. He is ashamed and enraged in equal measure.*

DOG-TAG: A party? He's at peace now, that marine. Celebrate? Like nothing's changed?

He remembers he's not at war right now, but that just confuses him—because war is what he knows

I can't be here. No-one understands. I can't be here! Is that okay, sir?

MUT-DOG: Why are you—? Are you / asking—?

DOG-TAG: I'm drowning, my lungs are— My— They are full of blood, other people's, and I'm drowning in there, but nobody even— Bubbling away in my chest—

He is exposed. He wants to either scream, cry or kill everyone in the room. Instead he takes a breath. Then another.

What am I meant to do now, sir?

Segue: Carlotta's bedroom.

CARLOTTA *is touching up the make-up on her face.*

CARLOTTA: Every morning I think tomorrow I'll get out. I started too late today.

Segue: The bar.

Everyone wants to disappear into the floorboards. Silence.

DOG-TAG: I need to go home now. I need to sleep. I need to—

MUT-DOG: Stand down, toy soldier. We thank you for your service.

DOG-TAG *exits.* CLIPPER *laughs, then almost cries. Everyone unravels slightly.*

CLIPPER: What a fuck-knuckle!

MUT-DOG: He is the bravest of us all.

SCENE EIGHT

Transition: Carlotta's house.

CARLOTTA *is touching up the make-up on her face.*

CARLOTTA: I started too late today. That's the problem. Have to attack it early. Before the thinking creeps in. What if someone recognises me? What if no-one recognises me? If I was—?

> CHIKA *is suddenly there, bloodied but bandaged. He holds a brown bag.* CARLOTTA *feels exposed and ugly.*

CHIKA: Home delivery.

CARLOTTA: I prefer back door / delivery.

CHIKA: Hey, beautiful. You don't get out anymore. We miss you at / the clubs.

CARLOTTA: Do I disgust you?

CHIKA: What? You're beautiful. Or what's your—? Fabulous!

CARLOTTA: I am hideous.

CHIKA: Fabulous, always and / forever.

CARLOTTA: No need for that, I know / what I am.

CHIKA: You're the only bloke I know that I love. And, mate, that ain't no / small feat.

CARLOTTA: You're sweet. People aren't sweet anymore. Oh, your beautiful face, my darling boy, what / happened?

CHIKA: A slight detour, but nothing would prevent me from— It's a gift from the old gang. / You never visit us anymore.

> CARLOTTA *touches his face. She kisses his cheek.* CHIKA's *heart is unexpectedly engaged in* CARLOTTA's *internal dilemma.*

I have MDMA, Angel Dust, Poppers, Snappers, Rock, Benzos, Cue Tips, Mud, Ritalin, Valium / Mesc, what's your—?

CARLOTTA: MDA. Yes. Yes. / I was young once—

> CHIKA *sexily takes a pill from his pockets and places it on her tongue. Beat. She swallows it. Silence. Lights go off in The Hell Room.* CHIKA *is gone.* CARLOTTA *is suddenly alone but experiencing an ecstasy trip.*

Carlotta stewing in her own juices.

CARLOTTA: At least I have my PMA.

The Hell Room is lit.

LOTTE: Ladies and gentleman, welcome back to The Hell Room, the vocal styling's of Carlotta, or as we all know her—Her Grand Mistress, Head of Cabbage!

> CARLOTTA *steps up to the microphone in her full glory. She is blowing kisses to the audience.*

CARLOTTA: Ladies and gentlemen. Cock suckers and clit lickers and mother fuckers all, come on in, come on in, come on in— Ha!

LOTTE: *Come on into The Hell Room.*

> CARLOTTA *blows out more kisses to the audience.*

CARLOTTA: The orchestra is beautiful. If you live in Siberia. Ha!

> *She positions herself centre stage. Indicates for the music to play.*

I ask myself again.
To be or not to be,
Six feet and bulletproof,
And broken heart, maybe.
Alone and empty flat,
With memories behind,
Carlotta wish you best,
Don't cry, my friend, don't cry.

I have my PMA,
To keep my life alive.
Carlotta feeling pain,
But subtle and sublime.
You question 'what the fuck?
This fucking PMA?'

My darling, wait, I will explain.
Positive Mental Attitude.
That keeps my hopes alive.
Carlotta feeling pain,
But she completely fine.
Life fuck me from behind,
From bottom and from top.
Carlotta looking forward.

For love and fuck and hope
For love and fuck and hope
For love and fuck and hope
For love and fuck and hope
For love and fuck and hope
For love and fuck and hope
For love and fuck and hope
For love and fuck and hope

Alone in empty flat,
With memories behind.
Carlotta wish you best,
Don't cry my friend, don't cry.

SCENE NINE

Transition: The bar.

CLIPPER *and* MUT-DOG *are together, but now alone.*

CLIPPER: You're a good kid, how is it you ended up on the streets?

MUT-DOG: Safer.

CLIPPER: Safer?

MUT-DOG: No men with their grabby paws all over me, sniff, sniff, / sniffing.

CLIPPER: Fuck, the world is fucked.

> *Silence.* CLIPPER *softens.*

Fuck, the world is…

> CLIPPER *takes a drink, and is relieved.*

MUT-DOG: Why drink?

CLIPPER: Sorry?

MUT-DOG: Tit for tat. Why drink?

CLIPPER: It's— Um, how can I—? Complicated.

MUT-DOG: I'm a brainiac, I understand complicated.

CLIPPER: I'm sure you do, it's me that— It's me that can't seem to— I'm the dickhead. Clearly.

MUT-DOG: I don't feel things, you know.

CLIPPER: You don't—?

MUT-DOG: Feel things.
CLIPPER: Good for you.
MUT-DOG: But I see things in 20/20.
CLIPPER: You—?
MUT-DOG: Crystal clear.

> *From the shadows:*

DOG-TAG: *Peace.*
PT: *Laughter.*
PEPPER: *Touch.*
CRYSTAL: *Love.*
GIZMO: *Happiness.*
CARLOTTA: *Sex.*

> CLIPPER *goes to take a drink.* MUT-DOG *stops him.*

MUT-DOG: I see things. You. I see / you.
CLIPPER: Don't. Please, don't.
MUT-DOG: Yes.

> *Silence.*

My mum lost me. Who lost you?
CLIPPER: How could you—? Me? Are you asking me?
MUT-DOG: I see things.
CLIPPER: Who lost—?
MUT-DOG: You can play hide and seek all you like in the drinky-drink, but at the end of the day, no-one is that thirsty.

> *Silence.*

CLIPPER: My wife. My wife. My wife.
MUT-DOG: Lost you?
CLIPPER: Forgot me.
MUT-DOG: My mum was a wife.
CLIPPER: My wife is a—

> *Beat.*

She looks at me like I'm a foreigner in her life. She fights me. I scare her because I'm no longer known to her. I'm a ghost in her own mind, like a memory that doesn't fit. Sometimes, I sort of just— I just wish she'd die. It would be so much— A blessing really.

MUT-DOG: My mum forgot me. Before the *taking* we laughed. After the *taking* she cried and cried until she was all cried out. Then I think she just forgot all about me. I need a piss.

   MUT-DOG *exits.* CLIPPER *holds up his drink.*

   LOTTE *is revealed in The Hell Room. She sings; her words infect* CLIPPER*'s consciousness. He is discovering this truth as he sings it.*

CLIPPER: I like the feel of it, in my hand. Don't really like the way it tastes, it's more that — A full glass feels optimistic.
LOTTE: *I like the feel of the scotch, it's rough / and it's hard.*
CLIPPER: I can't go to the club anymore. Too many eyes—
LOTTE: *I like the way its coldness / touches me.*
CLIPPER: The men all— Too many eyes—
LOTTE: *It smothers words and sentiment, it tastes so lonely,*
CLIPPER: I need the syrup, the rush to— I need the escape.
LOTTE: *I like the way it helps me not feel.*
CLIPPER: She's trapped in a trap— We're both trapped in this—
LOTTE: *I never liked the way it tastes;*
   It's sort of like a rusty old nail;
   I love the way it clings to the glass, /
   The way it just hangs in there.
CLIPPER: I need things to be fun again. A break from her— Her relentlessness.
LOTTE: *I'm most at ease when I got a drink, tightly in my hand,*
CLIPPER: I need my cock sucked.
LOTTE: *I'm comfortable, I'm safe, and I'm warm.*
   Like I could walk up to anyone, and just say 'Hello'.
CLIPPER: I want to get fucked. I need to fuck, to pound like a—?

   He wants to take a drink, but recognises his own cowardice and so he hesitates.

LOTTE: *Just ask them, 'Hey, how are you in there?'*

   CLIPPER *begins to break down.*

   Who am I?
CLIPPER: *I'm just someone, anyone,*
LOTTE: *No-one,*

BOTH: I'm okay, yeah sure, I'm doing fine.

> *Long silence. Music slowly kicks back in.*

CLIPPER: Life is great, why wouldn't it be, yeah, abso-fucking-lutely.

> *Lights in The Hell Room go black.*

I need my wife to remember me, one more time.

> CLIPPER *fights his demon, hoping to not take a drink. He loses the fight and takes a drink, shamefully and simultaneously relieved.*

Loneliness is caught with her pants down.

SCENE TEN

PEPPER *is sitting in the hole under The Hell Room, eating a can of baked beans. She addresses the audience directly.*

PEPPER: I hate baked beans. Hate everything about them. The smell. The texture. Even the idea of them. Hate them. Dog-food the lot if you ask me. And all of it has a shelf life, and once that's past, they feed it to us. May as well wear a sign on my forehead. Homeless. Charity case. But that's not the— Sorry. See, I don't want you to think I'm a whinger. I know we make our own lot in life and all, except we don't. Not all the way ourselves Not all the way. Shhh, this is— Not all the way. We can be tipped. She comes and whispers in our ears every now and again, and can tip us either way. I've seen it. Her. After they took my boy, I— I— It's hard to talk about—

> *She places the can down, rips off the tin lid, holds it to her wrist.*

Then I heard her.

> LOTTE *sings from the shadows.*

LOTTE: Where did he go, that fresh-faced kid in the family album?
Where, where did he go, where did he go?

PEPPER: And then I saw her.

> LOTTE *is illuminated as she sings.*

LOTTE: All gone wrong. All gone. Gone.

PEPPER: No!

LOTTE stops. They stare. LOTTE *moves and takes the tin from her hand.*

LOTTE: Here, this one's on the house.

> PEPPER *hesitates, as* LOTTE *slowly ties red ribbon on* PEPPER'*s wrists.*

Any last words?

> PEPPER *pulls away.*

PEPPER: You don't have the juice!

From the shadows:

DOG-TAG: *Rat-a-tat-ta.*
PT: *Thwack.*
CLIPPER: *Crash.*
CRYSTAL: *Puff.*
GIZMO: *Ka-ching!*
CARLOTTA: *Ha!*

> LOTTE *hisses, drops the tin lid and leaves.* PEPPER *regards her wrists.*

PEPPER: I didn't cut deep enough to— Just deep enough to see her. And now I see her everywhere. Hear her— Whispering. This is where it happened. This is where they found him whenever he'd run away — He hid here as a child when they— Hid under the floorboards, waiting for— Waiting. He was stolen from me and I— I fought but the courts, the laws were, are, were— Hide I taught him, hidey hide and— I sometimes feel like he's still here, just watching, just—

> *She begins to exit, stops and addresses the audience directly.*

Oh, by the way, why a tin lid from a can of baked beans? Because when they found my cupboards full of them— All out of date. Well, what sort of mother is that, eh?

> PEPPER *sits on the ground and rubs her wrist.*

> *All the characters are in their own worlds. Slowly one by one they all dissolve, except for* PEPPER *who remains on the street.*

> MUT-DOG *appears, and looks at her.* PEPPER *dissolves.*

MUT-DOG: I remember you I think, from before the *taking.*

Segue: CRYSTAL *is trying to light a cigarette. She is flicking the lighter, but it fails to catch light.*

CRYSTAL: Damn. Bugger. Shit. Shit, piss and fuck!

MUT-DOG: Before the—?

Loneliness has a smoko.

SCENE ELEVEN

Transition: CRYSTAL *trying to light a cigarette.*

CRYSTAL: Shit. Shit, piss and—

> *She shakes the lighter, and re-tries, but it fails to catch light.*

Fuck! Today isn't going to be a good / day.

> *The Hell Room is illuminated.*

Just let me have it, Dessie.
Light up the flame.
It fills me up,
It dulls the pain,
I don't care now, I have no shame,
Just let me have it, Dessie.

'Those things'll be the death of ya.'
Yeah, yeah.
Puff, puff.
That's pretty ironic, love.
'Those things'll be the death of ya.'
Yeah, yeah.
Puff, puff.
I buried my only love.

I'm hungry for it, I'm so empty now.
It takes me away.
To another time,
To another life,
When I was a wife...

Just let me have it, Dessie.
Light up the flame.

It fills me up,
It dulls the pain,
I don't care now, I have no shame,
Just let me have it, Dessie.

Loneliness may have been born at night, but it wasn't last night.

SCENE TWELVE

Transition: The characters are all revealed in their own worlds, in their isolation.

MUT-DOG *is looking through his bag.* PEPPER *is holding the empty wine bottle, lost in her pain.* GIZMO *is reading his form guide.* DOG-TAG *is being tormented by his demons.* CARLOTTA *is applying make-up.* CLIPPER *is watching his hands, as they tremble.* PT *is watching television. The lights slow to black on each character as they speak.*

DOG-TAG: Rat-a-tat-ta.
PT: Thwack.
PEPPER: Scratch.
CRYSTAL: Puff.
GIZMO: Ka-ching!
CARLOTTA: Ha!
CLIPPER: Shake.

> *The light lingers on* CLIPPER. *He shakes his hands to try and get them to stop shaking.*

Hard to tell really. My hands, used to be— Like a surgeon's, rock-steady, but now— Remember, sweetheart, the day of our wedding I was like a virgin at a whorehouse, scared senseless, but when I took your hand in mine and placed that ring— Remember—? Rock-steady when I had you right there beside— But—? Now, is it the jitters, or the rage at—? Maybe, anyway.

> *Silence, his wife (unseen) is staring out blankly, a victim of Alzheimer's.* CLIPPER *pulls out a couple of pill bottles from his jacket, and takes a couple out of each, his hands still shaking.*

It's time for your meds, sweetheart. Don't— Stop! Don't run away from me it's your medicine— I'm not— I'm not playing a game.

It's not hide and— Fuck! I'm trying to help you, you useless crazy, mad, fucking, fucking, fucking, fuck! I'm trying to fucking help!

He accidently throws the pills and pill bottles on the ground in a spasm of rage.

Stop laughing, it's not. Stop! Stop! It's not— For fuck's— You think this is funny? It's not funny. Stop. Look what I've— You think this is—? You do my head in with this—

CLIPPER is being softened by her laughter (unheard), a reminiscence of an earlier time. He almost giggles, despite himself. He is trying to maintain the role of parent, but failing.

It's not funny. You mad bitch. You crazy, magnificent, beautiful, beautiful, mad bit—

His heart breaks. He falls to the ground, literally felled by his love for her.

I love you so much. Too much. Too— Too—

SCENE THIRTEEN

Loneliness mops up the spilt milk.

Transition: The soup kitchen.

PEPPER is sitting there with her bowl of cereal. CHIKA enters, his hands bandaged. He sits next to PEPPER.

PEPPER: It's a beautiful morning.

CHIKA: It is. It's a beautiful morning, if you like room searches and caseworkers crawling up your arse and down into your lower bowel for a drug test.

PEPPER: Oh, Chika, how you talk. This needs sugar or salt. I can't be sure which. What happened to you?

CHIKA: What always happens to me, I got fucked up.

PEPPER: When will you ever learn?

CHIKA: How long is a piece of string?

PEPPER: Too long.

CHIKA is struggling to eat his soup because his hands are bandaged.

Here, you're worse than a child. Let me.

PEPPER *begins to feed* CHIKA *his soup, alternating between feeding him and her. He remains guileless.*

CHIKA: When I was a kid, the world used to terrify me. Every time adults got together and talked it seemed to be getting worse. There were too many people on the planet so we were going to run out of room. There wouldn't be enough food for everyone either, so we'd all become cannibals. There was a hole in the ozone that we couldn't patch up. Acid rain was killing the forests. The Great Barrier Reef was dying. Everything could give you cancer. The oil was going to run out and to top it off we would all die in a nuclear accident, like Chernobyl.

PEPPER: I think salt. Chika, / hand me the salt.

CHIKA *does so. She sprinkles some into their bowls, continues feeding.*

CHIKA: None of that happened, but still— Fear is I met this guy, the guy that did this. Like a child, but with no fear and it made me— All the drugs, all the booze and pills, I've never been fearless like that. It terrified me.

PEPPER: Maybe some pepper, / Chika, could you?

CHIKA *does so.*

CHIKA: He smiles at me while he's beating the fuck out of me. Just keeps smiling, like he knows something I don't, which—

PEPPER: There's something about this soup that's just— / Wrong?

CHIKA: So I smile at him. I smile back, and it kind of— He stops, and is looking at me. And I see, in that moment I see something flicker. Behind his eyes, like a tear, just a hint of a— He stops beating the bejesus out of me and says—

MUT-DOG & CHIKA: *Sorry, I had to stop all your screaming.*

CHIKA: And he starts to walk away, but not before giving me the biggest handkerchief I have ever—

PEPPER: Do people still carry / handkerchiefs?

CHIKA: I am so, so, so sick of everybody blaming their disease or their life's dive down the s-bend on their issues. Everyone saying you get the disease you deserve, that karma shit or whatever the—? There's a real lie in the middle of all that, and I bought in hook, line and— Don't get me— I bought in and dropped out, I thought, fuck this shit, I'm no victim, but the fact is— Well, the truth is— What happened— I'm the victim. I'm the dropkick and I didn't even know it, but inside, inside I've been fucking screaming, just as frightened as Mr Corduroy!

PEPPER: We're all silently screaming.

CHIKA: Some of us, not so silently.

From the shadows:

MUT-DOG: *Sorry, I had to— Sorry.*

    CHIKA *dry retches.*

CHIKA: Hey, you're right, this soup is

PEPPER: Yeah but free.

    CHIKA *stands.*

You off?

CHIKA: Nah, getting bread rolls, a man's gotta eat.

PEPPER: The carbs coma, eh?

CHIKA: Means I can sleep the day away.

PEPPER: I know, of course I know.

CHIKA: Better to sleep than face— Better to sleep.

Pepper hands him her bowl, which he takes it and exits.

Segue: the street Mut-Dog appears, he is happy. He howls.

Segue: the Soup Kitchen.

PEPPER *hands him her bowl, which he takes and exits.*

PEPPER: Yes, indeed.

SCENE FOURTEEN

Transition: MUT-DOG *rushes into The Hell Room. He sings:*

MUT-DOG: *Lego Rockets, Dogs called Sproket,*
  Butch, Spot, Fido, Patch,
  Drooling Tongues, Panting Lungs,
  Lie down get Fleas—Scratch!

  Don't like People,
  Don't feel Anything,

Dogs are Loyal,
Canine Best Friend.
Makes me Sing!

Food in Bins, Yum din-dins,
Share it with me Mate,
Dog Boy Heaven, One day's Seven,
Pizza Box for Plate.

Don't like People,
Don't feel Anything,
Dogs are Loyal,
Canine Best Friend.
Makes me Sing!

Wanting Needing, Taunting Teasing,
Who needs Rules and Lies,
Rolling Yelping, Pack-Pup Helping,
Wet Noses—Honest Eyes.
Don't like People,
Don't feel Anything,
Dogs are Loyal,
Canine Best Friend.
Makes me—

    MUT-DOG *howls.*

SCENE FIFTEEN

Transition: PT *is sitting watching children's television. He slowly pulls out an envelope, he knows what it is but is avoidant.*

PT: A letter? Not from the kids, I—? No, not them. Official. No drawings for daddy? No drawing's for Daddy today. No drawings for—

    He is opening a letter from the courts. The lights go on in The Hell Room. He is reading and crying.

Married? Married? Full— Full custody—? They are still my kids. My— My— I'm no joke. I'm no. Fuck!

    LOTTE *sings.* PT *starts to rub at the make-up on his face, it is all getting distorted.*

LOTTE: *Now what am I doing here?*
  Sometimes it doesn't make sense to me
  As I sit here in my armchair,
  Looking out at all the debris,
  But I won't give it up,
  I'm ready to give it a go,
  I'm ready to say 'no', to trouble.
  Say no, no, no, no, no.

> *As the music plays,* LOTTE *riffs. It fuels* PT*'s anger. He tears up the letter. He throws himself around the room, finally falling down. He howls.*

To trouble, Say no, no, no, no, no.

SCENE SIXTEEN

Transition: The bar.

CLIPPER *and* GIZMO *are sitting there.* DOG-TAG *in his chair.*

GIZMO: You didn't shave today?

CLIPPER: I—? What—?

GIZMO: Looks like you didn't / shave today.

CLIPPER: I did. Of course, what you think I—? Think I'm losing / my mind?

GIZMO: It's a strange idea though, / isn't it?

CLIPPER: What are you—?

GIZMO: Shaving.

CLIPPER: Are you kidding me with this / shit?

GIZMO: All I'm saying is—

CLIPPER: Fuck you.

GIZMO: By nature. Men have hair. You don't think to shave your chest or / scrotum, do you?

CLIPPER: Hair is dead.

GIZMO: So who decided that / we need to shave?

CLIPPER: Dead tissue. Yes, it keeps on keeping on, always there, it looks as if it's growing, but it's just— It's excrement. We scrape it off with a razor because it's disgusting. It's dead, looks like it's alive, but she's not, not really. Not her / anymore.

GIZMO: Her?

CLIPPER: What? Sorry?

GIZMO: You said her.

CLIPPER: Don't tell me what I— I know what I said.

GIZMO: You said her.

CLIPPER: Listen, because this is—? Listen. Just because a person says something, doesn't mean jackshit! People say things all the time, with no intention of meaning it. Of sticking to their word. That's from another era. Another time.

GIZMO: Sticking to your / word?

CLIPPER: Vows. Pledges. The idea that things last. Nothing lasts, so why—?

GIZMO: So why shave?

CLIPPER: We get smaller and smaller until we just—

Segue: CARLOTTA, *in her room, opening a letter.*

CARLOTTA: I never expected a letter. Someone wrote. How very Oscar Wilde. Darling, let me kiss you like a lady. Thank you, darling.

Segue: The public bar.

GIZMO: I don't mind getting smaller. It fits me. It's comfortable. Here's my little patch, and it suits me / just fine.

CLIPPER: For years, I've kept everyone just there. At arm's length. Just there. Never turned my back, and never let that arm down. Kept everyone right there. The kids. My wife. Everyone right there. Just—

SCENE SEVENTEEN

Transition: LOTTE *enters as* CARLOTTA *puts lipstick on her lips. She then preens himself in the mirror.*

LOTTE: It's a beautiful morning.

CARLOTTA: Thrilling. You're not dead yet, gorgeous.

She kisses the envelope as she opens it. She pulls out a business letter.

What the—?

LOTTE: It is, it is, it is, it is, it is, it is a beautiful morning. Let's check your phone.

She moves to the phone.

You have no messages.

As she laughs, CARLOTTA *finds a cheque attached to the letter.*

LOTTE *sings:*

It's a beautiful morning.

CARLOTTA *unstaples the cheque and it falls to the ground.*

Oh, do share.

CARLOTTA *is reading the letter.* LOTTE *is over her shoulder reading it too.*

CARLOTTA: Since we had had no responses to your request to join RSVP after three months / we've got a policy for—

LOTTE *laughs.*

A refund?

LOTTE *picks up the cheque.*

LOTTE: What's this? You have no-one. Can't even buy love. No-one at all.

She laughs, rips up the cheque, and sings and throws the ripped cheque above CARLOTTA*'s head. She grabs* CARLOTTA *and spins her around.*

I have my PMA,
To keep my life alive.
Carlotta feeling pain,
But subtle and sublime.

CARLOTTA: *Enough!*

She strips out of her 'gown', until exposed as a man in his underwear.

I am what I am. And what I am, is a middle-aged man.

Loneliness takes the day off.

LOTTE *moves to* CARLOTTA, *and together they take off his make-up and dress him in a suit, as she sings.*

LOTTE: *I was walking one day, through fields of grey.*
Birds are humming, some care to say,

Why aren't we flying, flying away?
Why aren't we flying, flying away?
Some are lonely, looking up seeing freedom
But never knowing it.
CARLOTTA: *Why aren't we flying, flying away?*
Some are lonely, looking up seeing freedom,
LOTTE: *But never knowing it.*
Some are lonely, looking up seeing freedom, but never knowing it.
Some are lonely, looking up seeing freedom, but never knowing it.
Some are lonely, looking up seeing freedom, but never knowing it.
Freedom. Freedom. Freedom

> CARLOTTA *is now fully dressed as a man.*

> *Segue:* DOG-TAG *is at his table.*

DOG-TAG: I thought the dead didn't talk. Stop talking to me stop talking to me stop talking to me stop talking to me stop talking stop talking stop!

> *Segue: Carlotta's bedroom. He is singing with* LOTTE.

BOTH: *Freedom. Freedom. Freedom.*

SCENE EIGHTEEN

Transition: Dog-Tag's room. He is tormented.

DOG-TAG: I was told I was fighting for my country. I was fighting for my country in someone else's country, and they were— Well. They were *actually fighting for their country.*

Loneliness pokes the pig until it squeals.

> LOTTE *is revealed in The Hell Room.* DOG-TAG *is in a suicidal frenzy.*

DOG-TAG: I was captured. By a boy. Thirteen. Maybe twelve. Fuck, maybe ten. Me and my staff sergeant both of us and— After months, they pulled out a video camera, gave him and me both iron bars and said, 'We don't have enough supplies to keep you both alive so decide'. And fuck me but I took that pipe and—

> DOG-TAG *is visibly shaken. To kill himself or someone else, he remains ambivalent.*

LOTTE: *Where did he go, that fresh-faced kid in the family album?*
Where, where did he go, where did he go?

DOG-TAG: What are my orders? I don't know what to do now. How to—?
Where are my orders? I need to get back there. To my men. To my—?
To—?

> DOG-TAG *stumbles to The Hell Room.*

LOTTE: Ladies and gentleman, please welcome one of our most decorated
and deserving returned soldiers after two tours, a three-year tour in
Iraq and a fifteen-month tour in Afghanistan. Yesterday's Hero—
Dog-Tag!

> DOG-TAG *awkwardly begins to sing.*

DOG-TAG: *I did what I was trained to do.*
I did what I was told, I did what I was told.
I fought for survival for my mates, for my country, for my country
And now the horror torments me.
Day and night, day and night.
If this is my fate, it's a fate worse than death.
The lives I destroyed, they have their revenge.

Hell Head. Hell Head. Hell Head. Hell Head.
The lives that I destroyed, they have their revenge.
Hell Head. Hell Head. Hell Head. Hell Head.
The lives that I destroyed, they have their revenge.

I did what I was trained to do.
I did what I was told, I did what I was told.
I fought for survival for my mates, for my country, for my country
And now the horror torments me.
Day and night, day and night.

Hell Head. Hell Head. Hell Head. Hell Head.
The lives that I destroyed, they have their revenge.
Hell Head. Hell Head. Hell Head. Hell Head.
The lives that I destroyed, they have their revenge.

> DOG-TAG *stumble back to his room.*

DOG-TAG: The lives that I destroyed, they have their revenge.

LOTTE: Trying to punch out a couple of zeds, baby?

Segue: the hotel.

GIZMO *is holding a cup cake, with a candle in it.*

GIZMO: Not everyone's a winner. Gotta factor the odds.

GIZMO *lights the cup cake.*

Segue: DOG-TAG *runs to his chair, opens the tin on his table, is disgusted by his fall from grace / puts it away again.*

LOTTE: Rat-a-tat-tat!

DOG-TAG *is clearly distressed, he paces.*

Segue: the hotel.

GIZMO: So, happy birthday to me.

Segue: The chair.

DOG-TAG *is trying to reposition it.*

LOTTE: Oh, you've really cracked the sads, haven't you, soldier? Well, drink some concrete and harden the fuck up!

DOG-TAG *is clearly distressed. He sits down, but remains agitated.*

Rat-a-tat-tat!

GIZMO: Who do you think—? You're kidding, you complete—!

GIZMO *blows out the candle.*

Segue: The chair.

DOG-TAG *starts counting out in his head and on his fingers, working out the odds, he is muttering to himself as he does this.* LOTTE *yawns.*

DOG-TAG: The lives I've destroyed will have their—

LOTTE *opens the tin and hands* DOG-TAG *a hand gun.*

Segue: The soup kitchen.

CHIKA *is there.* CRYSTAL *enters with some more cereal.*

Loneliness white-knuckles it.

CRYSTAL: You boys want any more / cereal?

CHIKA *lifts his bowl in the air, and* CRYSTAL *tips some in.*

No more milk, though.

CHIKA *shrugs and starts eating.*

Segue: Dog-Tag's room.

DOG-TAG: One last mission.

DOG-TAG *holds the gun in his hand, and slowly lifts it to his mouth. Lights fade on* DOG-TAG.

SCENE NINETEEN

Transition: The soup kitchen.

CRYSTAL: Coming up to the silly season.

CHIKA: Thanks for the grub, Mrs.

CRYSTAL: Oh, call me Crystal. And you are?

CHIKA: Chika.

She goes to shake his hand, he takes her hand and kisses it. She is overwhelmed; no man has kissed her since Des, even on the hands. It devastates her.

CRYSTAL: Why did you—? Why would you—? Oh? Why? What gives / you the—?

CHIKA: Just because I'm poor now doesn't mean I can't afford any manners. A lady deserves respect. You come here, out of your day, to help feed us. To listen to us. To let us know we are not alone.

CRYSTAL: Darling, all I do is slop the slop on a plate and serve.

CHIKA: Most people do a lot less. You think we don't notice? We notice.

CRYSTAL: Actually, get's me out of the house, should have volunteered years ago. But thanks for saying— You're sweet.

Silence. She remembers what it is to be loved.

You remind me of my Des. Heart of gold. He'd give you the shirt off his back. In fact, he did, the silly bugger. Had our own little pharmacy shop at The Cross. All the druggies would come in, with all sorts of troubles. Could never afford their medication though, so he'd just hand it over. 'When you get on your feet you can pay me back.' You'd be surprised how many did come back too. Maybe not pay him everything though owed, but that wasn't— Paid what they could. / Real decent.

CHIKA: I think I remember him, did he always sit out the front smoking old Camels? And that old hat with the fishing / hooks in it.

> CRYSTAL *laughs.*

CRYSTAL: He was a character, that's for sure. Never went fishing a day in his life.

CHIKA: Do you still own it?

CRYSTAL: What—? Oh, no. I work in the carpark under the Westfield shopping centre.

CHIKA: Must be getting busy this time of year.

CRYSTAL: Don't get me started. Rude, the lot of them. Not like you boys. Tempers that could light the Martin Place Christmas tree. Not much Christmas spirit going there. Some even have the bad manners to blame *me* for *them* taking too long in the shops. I hate to say it and people don't like to hear it but 'I don't make the rules, do I?'

CHIKA: You're giving them a service.

CRYSTAL: Exactly.

> *Pause.*

I do love that Christmas tree in Martin Place. Have you seen it? / It's huge.

CHIKA: Sure.

CRYSTAL: I haven't had my own tree for years and years now. Ever since Des died, the bugger. Well, for starters, he used to drive out of town to get a real big old tree himself. Always said the country trees lasted longer, but they all turned brown come January first, if you ask me. Still, we'd decorate it together and— Well.

> *Silence.*

Oh well, the point is I love the Martin Place Christmas tree. I love seeing the faces of the children. So precious. So very precious.

CHIKA: Sorry for your loss.

CRYSTAL: Thanks, darls.

> *Pause.*

Let's see if I can't rustle up some more milk for you boys. Back in a jiff.

> CRYSTAL *exits. A gunshot is heard.* DOG-TAG *is dead. From the shadows:*

PT: *Thwack.*
CLIPPER: *Crash.*
CRYSTAL: *Puff.*
GIZMO: *Ka-ching!*
CARLOTTA: *Ha!*

Loneliness plays with the cattle.

SCENE TWENTY

Transition: Everyone is suddenly revealed in their own worlds.

The street: PT *is standing there in his clown make-up. He is trying to juggle, but keeps dropping the balls.*

The Century Hotel, public bar: GIZMO *is holding his form guide watching the TV above, he keeps losing.*

The soup kitchen: CHIKA *is eating his soup at the table. The street:*

CRYSTAL *is crying,* CLIPPER *walks up and hands her a handkerchief. She smiles.*

CRYSTAL: Oh, I must look a right state.
CLIPPER: Only on the inside.
CRYSTAL: What a— What a thing to say.
CLIPPER: All our insides are pits of despair and pain. Best to just get on.
CRYSTAL: I always say—? I say that.
CLIPPER: Really?
CRYSTAL: All the— Yes, all the bleeding—
CLIPPER: Of course, it's crap, there is no getting on.
CRYSTAL: Absolute crap. I say it for /
BOTH: The others.
CRYSTAL: To make them feel / better.
CLIPPER: Good, / yes.
CRYSTAL: Yes.
CLIPPER: And what shit's me, more than anything, is /
BOTH: It does.
CRYSTAL: Yes, they feel better. Relieved.
CLIPPER: Off the fucking hook.
CRYSTAL: Yes.
CLIPPER: But they aren't the one on the fucking /

BOTH: Hook.

CLIPPER: In the first place. Right.

CRYSTAL: And you're left hanging.

CLIPPER: Like a—? Like a—?

CRYSTAL: Wet fish.

They laugh. Silence. Something falls away and they breathe together.

CLIPPER: Is there anything I can do? I mean, if there is I'd—

CRYSTAL: My husband's dead, and I still love— I still—

She takes a significant breath, breathing in her husband.

So there's nothing / to be done.

CLIPPER: I want my wife dead, because I still love her, but because of that there's really—

CRYSTAL: Nothing to be done.

CLIPPER *breathes out his wife: it's relief and devastation in equal measure.*

Is it cancer? If it is, I—? The pain is— The blind, numbing pain / is—

CLIPPER: Alzheimer's.

Silence. From the shadows

PT: *I'm forgetting the sound of your laughter, / my children.*

CHIKA: *It's all so terrifying, being safe.*

GIZMO: *Where is everyone gone?*

CARLOTTA: *I'm walking out that door and into newness.*

PEPPER: *I lost my own child.*

Silence.

CLIPPER: She's not even sixty years of— Not even—

CRYSTAL *hands back the handkerchief to* CLIPPER.

CRYSTAL: I'm so, so, sorry. My husband's mum had it something terrible. Yes, well— No matter how you cut it, it stinks to high heaven. Nothing to be said really.

CLIPPER: There's no word for someone like me, whose wife has forgotten—

CRYSTAL: No. No. At least my Des still knew who I was, although not sure that was any real comfort, to be honest.

Silence.

What a pair / of—

Silence. CLIPPER *reaches out to her.*

CLIPPER: I thought I was the only one, and it's been making me so furious
at—

CRYSTAL: The only one who—?

CLIPPER: Who knows what it means to— To—? To—?

CRYSTAL: Love?

> CLIPPER *begins to emotionally collapse,* CRYSTAL *moves in.*
> *Together they support each other, opening their hearts not to*
> *the other but their own self. They stop and look to each other, a*
> *connection is made.*

CLIPPER: I'm quite the arsehole.

CRYSTAL: I'm quite the bitch.

> *Pause.*

CLIPPER: How about I take you for a drink?

CRYSTAL: Oh, I'd really appreciate that. Thank you. A nice cup of tea.

CLIPPER: Oh—! Yes, sure. Actually, I would really like that. A cup of tea.
Like civilised people. Shall we—?

CRYSTAL: Crystal.

CLIPPER: People call me Clipper.

CRYSTAL: And you let them get away with that shit?

> CLIPPER *takes* CRYSTAL *by the arm.*

SCENE TWENTY-ONE

Transition.

Segue: The street.

MUT-DOG *is there.* PEPPER *enters.*

PEPPER: I've seen you about, but you don't seem to / like people.

MUT-DOG: Dogs are good, because they don't care how you smell.

PEPPER: Yes.

MUT-DOG: How do you make someone care about you? Dogs care.
Without even knowing you. They care. Why can't people be more
like dogs?

PEPPER: I know plenty of people who behave like a pack of—
MUT-DOG: They don't smell like dog. That's the real comfort.
PEPPER: It's okay, I won't bite, / love.
MUT-DOG: I might.

    Beat.

I don't feel things, you know.
PEPPER: Sometimes I think that would be a real blessing, to not feel /
    anything.
MUT-DOG: You'd be wrong.

    Silence.

PEPPER: You remind me of, I don't know.
MUT-DOG: A dog?
PEPPER: The past.
MUT-DOG: Part of me was fingers criss-crossed hoping that I remind you
    of a dog. Maybe a golden retriever, they're my / favourite.
PEPPER: Fingers criss-crossed?
MUT-DOG: You want some pizza? It's secondhand, but first-mouth if
    you get / my meaning.
PEPPER: Fingers crossed?
MUT-DOG: It's something mamma and I used / to pretend a wishbone on.

    PEPPER *looks deeply into* MUT-DOG*'s eyes, it makes him wriggly*
    squirm.

PEPPER: Sorry, but— Sorry. Sorry, but—

    Silence.

What's your name?
MUT-DOG: People call me Mut-Dog.
PEPPER: People call you—? Mut—?
MUT-DOG: Oh, they changed it— Different foster homes all had different
    names for me. Usually I was *Pet.* Like a pet.

    Silence.

So, Mut-Dog. Before then, I think—? Clear away the cobwebs and
shaky-shake the memory bulb, and—? Nothing.
PEPPER: Nothing?
MUT-DOG: All I can do is think. I don't feel things, you know.

PEPPER: Sorry, did you say you don't feel / things? Is it—?
MUT-DOG: It's how I remember it, before the *taking*, / it's how I remember—
PEPPER: Before the—? What?
MUT-DOG: The *taking*. I was stolen from my—
PEPPER: The taking?

> PEPPER *is hopeful.*

Sorry, but before the—? The—? The—?

SCENE TWENTY-TWO

Transition: LOTTE *is illuminated in The Hell Room.*

LOTTE: *Well there you go, and here we are,*
Whether from the gutter or Bellevue Hill we can all see the stars,
Dog-Tag's up there, looking down on us,
Rest in peace, Dog-Tag, I hope we were worth the fuss.

And here we are, and there you go,
Got a bone to pick? Or one of contention to throw?
Well, I ain't fetching—no dry bones!
You see my family here we got enough crossbones.

Oooooh, baby, something's got to give,
C'mon, c'mon, baby, we're just trying to live.

Well, there you go and here I am,
C'mon and take me by the hand,
Here we are and now you know
That none of us, none of us, want to let go.

So hold me, baby, squeeze me, baby,
Never ever let go.
Yeah, hold me, baby, love me, baby,
I want the world to know.

'Cause this is life,
This is love,
To live it you got to be fearless.
That's the story of life,
It's the glory of love ,
And to love, you've got to be fearless.

EPILOGUE

Lights up on the audience—100 per cent for two seconds. Blackout.

Lights slowly up on stage (not The Hell Room). DOG-TAG *lays dead, collapsed in an up-ended chair, with blood over this face, the gun by his side. The lights flicker on him for a few seconds, like a globe about to burst. Something shatters.*

Characters are revealed in their own worlds, around DOG-TAG*'s body, but not aware of him.*

PT: *Hey, it's Dad.*
CRYSTAL: *Ah.*
PEPPER: *Step.*
MUT-DOG: *Jump.*
CLIPPER: *Ask.*
CARLOTTA: *Yes.*
CHIKA: *Fear less.*
GIZMO: *Ka-ching!*
PEPPER: *Reach out.*
MUT-DOG: *Jump.*
CRYSTAL: *Ah.*
PT: *I miss you both.*
CARLOTTA: *Now.*
GIZMO: *Ka-ching!*
PT: *I belong to you.*

Lights snap to black on all but DOG-TAG.

From the blackness we hear:

CRYSTAL & CLIPPER: *What's stopping us from beginning?*

The lights flicker on DOG-TAG *for a few seconds, like a globe that's about the burst, something shatters. Lights snap to black.*

THE END